Wake, Sleepy One

CALIFORNIA POPPIES AND THE SUPER BLOOM

WRITTEN BY LISA KERR

ILLUSTRATED BY LISA POWELL BRAUN

WEST
MARGIN
PRESS

In the desert, a winter frost melts.
Fog drifts. Ravens cry.
Scorpions glow. Painted ladies glide.
Something new is about to begin.

Wake, sleepy one.

In the 1700s, early Spanish settlers came to California,
where they saw golden hillsides covered in poppies.
They called the flower "cupa de oro" ("golden cup") and
"dormidera" ("sleepy one") because of how it closes up at night.

A poppy seed wakes from a long winter's nap.
She drinks in the rain until full.
Crack, crack, crack.

POP!
A root runs deep.

Rise, sleepy one.

A seed that is dormant is asleep. California poppy seeds can lie dormant for many years. To wake up, or germinate, a seed needs water, warmth, and oxygen. In the desert, a poppy seed gets water from rainfall, underground moisture, or frost on the ground.

A single flower enters the world,
bursting out of the ground.

A California poppy bud is enclosed inside a hat-like
cover called a calyx. When the flower blooms and
the petals open up, the calyx falls off.

Stretching toward the sky,
the poppy's nightcap falls off.

Reach, sleepy one.

Wound tight, her petals point
straight to the sun.
Her arms cling to her sides like a
tiny dancer waiting in the wings.
Poppy is awake.

Wait, sleepy one.

After the calyx falls off, its petals remain tightly shut and pointed up at the sky. The flower unwinds slowly, but only when conditions are ideal.

The California poppy is unique because weather can affect if it stays open or closes back up. If the weather turns rainy or cold, the poppy will shut its petals.

A strong wind blows.
Poppy shivers.
A heavy rain falls.
A mouse darts along
the path to hide.

Fold, sleepy one.

A rattlesnake curls up.
Raindrops glide off its scales
and slip, slip, slide down its back.
Cactus roots collect water.
The desert wakes to drink.

Ready, sleepy one?

Many desert plants and animals have adaptations to help them survive. Rain is rare, so getting water can be a challenge. The Mojave rattlesnake curls up like a bowl. After it rains, the snake can drink from its own body.

Dark clouds roll away.
The sun shines on the Mojave.
Poppy's petals open wide,
revealing a golden cup.

Unfold, sleepy one.

After a storm, when the wind has calmed and the weather is warm again, the California poppy reopens to reveal four petals that form a small cup. Inside the cup are stamens and a pistil, which are the flower's reproductive organs.

Poppy takes center stage.
She stands alone,
a single orange flower,
brightening the drab desert floor.

A California poppy's petals have a special type of cell that creates a prism-like color effect. This gives the flower its intense orange glow and makes the petals look silky. Scientists think this helps attract pollinators like bees.

Her petals flutter softly in the breeze.
She balances on a delicate stem...
...swirling, swirling, swirling.

Dance, bright one.

Crack, crack, crack.
POP!
Nearby, another poppy wakes,
reaches for the sky, and begins...
          ...twirling, twirling, twirling.
Crack, crack.
Pop, pop.

And another and another...
Crack, pop, spin and twirl.
Crack, pop, spin, unfurl.
At last, it's time for...

Only with the perfect amount of rain and warmth will native desert flowers sprout and bloom.
In the Mojave Desert blooming begins in March, peaks in April, and ends by early summer.

...the *super bloom!*

When an unusually high number of dormant seeds wake up at the same time, it's called a "super bloom."
Super blooms can happen anywhere in the world, but in California it typically happens every ten years on average.

A sea of orange awakens,
swaying back and forth like waves.
Purple, yellow, white, and green join in.
All the colors of the desert come to life.

Bees buzz. Beetles high-step.
Butterflies land. Roadrunners race.

Shimmer, bright ones.

Although fans of the California desert super bloom often focus on the beautiful California poppy,
there are lots of other wildflowers, plants, and animals that join in to celebrate these special conditions.

The sun fades and the moon slides high.
A cool blue blanket wraps around the desert.
Owls hunt. Coyotes howl.
Red-tailed hawks settle into trees.
Squirrels burrow.

Rest, sleepy one.

People think of the desert as an empty place, but life is everywhere.
Many animals, like owls and coyotes, are nocturnal and come out only at
night to hunt and forage. Others, like red-tailed hawks and white-tailed
antelope squirrels, are diurnal and prefer the daytime, no matter the heat.

Poppy and the other flowers curl up,
hiding the sea of gold...

...until tomorrow.

Goodnight, sleepy one.

"Sleepy one" is the perfect nickname for the California poppy, and this is why: every evening the flower curls up its petals and closes them tightly, just like it's going to bed. This behavior is called nyctinasty.

GLOSSARY

adaptation: the ability to make changes in order to survive

botanist: a scientist who studies plants

calyx: a green "hat" made from two joined sepals that protects the flower bud

diurnal: describes an animal or plant that is active only during the day

dormant: a seed that is asleep

Mojave: the Mojave Desert, an arid area that spans part of southeastern California, southern Nevada, and some of Arizona and Utah

nocturnal: describes an animal or plant that is active only at night

nyctinasty: refers to a plant's response to darkness

petal: the part of a flower that protects a plant's reproductive parts

pistil: female reproductive organ of a flower

sepal: a leaf-like element of the calyx which encloses the petals

stamen: male reproductive organ of a flower

stem: the part of the plant that supports the leaves, roots, and flowers

taproot: a root that runs longer and deeper than other roots

torus: a ring that looks like a collar, which sits at the top of the stem

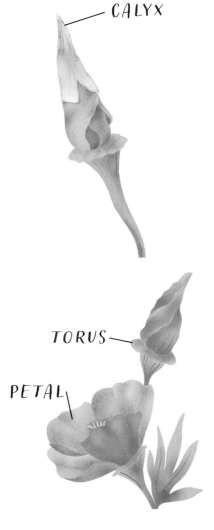

CALYX

TORUS

PETAL

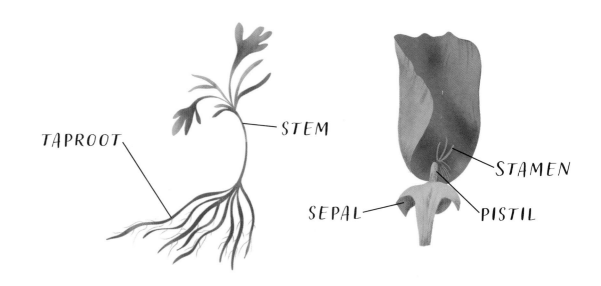

TAPROOT

STEM

STAMEN

SEPAL

PISTIL

MORE ABOUT CALIFORNIA POPPIES

Four hundred years before we started enjoying the super bloom, Indigenous Peoples used (and still use) the poppy as food and medicine, and to help with sleep. German botanist Adelbert von Chamisso first cataloged the California poppy in 1816 in the San Francisco Bay Area. He named it *Eschscholzia californica* for his friend Dr. Johann Eschscholtz, who he met on a Russian expedition ship. Ten years later the seeds were sent to the Royal Botanical Society in England. After that, poppies began growing in gardens all around the world.

In 1890, botanist Sarah Plummer Lemmon suggested the poppy for California's state flower, but it took her thirteen years to convince the state government. She succeeded in 1903 and a century later they declared April 6th to be California Poppy Day!

MORE ABOUT THE SUPER BLOOM

Every spring wildflowers bloom, but for the event to be a "super bloom" the right amounts of warmth and rain are needed to encourage an enormous amount of seeds to grow. A super bloom doesn't occur very often, but when it does, it's so bright and colorful that astronauts can even see it from space! Other beautiful flowers like the Joshua tree bloom, owl's clover, lupine, fiddleneck, goldfield, cream cups, and red maids also bloom with the poppy during the super bloom in California.

PROTECT THE SUPER BLOOM!

The areas where super blooms happen are fragile. They can be easily destroyed by visitors who want to admire their beauty. Protected and endangered wildlife can also be disturbed. You can keep super blooms going for generations to come by following some simple steps:

1. Stay on the marked foot trails.
2. Don't jump over fences or cross marked boundaries.
3. Use designated photo spots. If there aren't any, stay on the trail when taking photos.
4. Pack out any trash that you bring in.
5. Don't pick the flowers or bother wildlife.
6. Follow all park rules and directions.

FIND BLOOMS NEAR YOU

Super blooms are rare and don't always happen twice in the same spot.
Although it's difficult to guess when and where the next super bloom
will be, here are some great places to look for wildflowers blooming every year.

CALIFORNIA

- Antelope Valley California Poppy Reserve
- Anza-Borrego Desert State Park
- Carrizo Plain National Monument
- Chino Hills State Park
- Coyote Hills Regional Park
- Death Valley National Park (CA & NV)
- Diamond Valley Lake
- Joshua Tree National Park
- Mojave Trails National Monument
- Mount Davidson Park
- Point Mugu State Park
- Point Pinole Regional Shoreline
- Point Reyes National Seashore
- Russian Ridge Preserve
- Santa Monica Mountains National Recreation Area
- Walker Canyon Ecological Reserve

ARIZONA

- Alamo Lake State Park
- Catalina State Park
- Lost Dutchman State Park
- Oracle State Park
- Picacho Peak State Park
- Saguaro National Park
- Red Rock State Park

NEVADA

- Death Valley National Park (CA & NV)
- Lake Mead National Recreation Area
- Red Rock Canyon National Conservation Area
- Valley of Fire State Park

NEW MEXICO

- White Sands National Monument

OREGON

- The Cove Palisades State Park

UTAH

- Zion National Park
- Snow Canyon State Park

Here are more resources to help find wildflower displays near you:

America's State Parks: www.stateparks.org

Wildflowers of North America: www.inaturalist.org/projects/wildflowers-of-north-america

U.S. Forest Service Wildflower Viewing Areas: www.fs.fed.us/wildflowers/viewing

ANTELOPE BUTTE TRAIL
ANTELOPE TRAIL
SOUTH LOOP   1.1 MI
ANTELOPE TRAIL
NORTH LOOP   1.8 MI
Please STAY ON TRAIL

POPPY PIONEER: JANE PINHEIRO

One of the staunchest protectors of California poppies and their fragile desert ecosystem was Jane Pinheiro. Known as the "Poppy Lady," Pinheiro was a self-taught botanist and watercolor artist who painted local plants. She was upset to see people invading natural lands where Joshua trees, poppies, and other wildflowers thrived, so in 1960 she started fighting to protect it. By 1964, she had helped create nine wildlife and wildflower sanctuaries.

Pinheiro also raised money alongside the Lancaster Women's Club with a statewide school fundraiser called "Pennies for Poppies." In 1976, she raised enough money to buy 1,800 acres, which became the Antelope Valley California Poppy Reserve, also called "Poppy Park." Visitors from around the world travel there to walk the miles of wildflower trails. Pinheiro died in 1978, and four years later the Jane S. Pinheiro Interpretive Center opened in the park and now houses many of her beautiful wildflower paintings.

READ MORE

Deresti Betik, Lisa, and Josh Holinaty. *In the Dark: the Science of What Happens at Night.* Toronto, ON: Kids Can Press, 2020.

Stewart, Jon Mark. *Mojave Desert Wildflowers: A Field Guide to High Desert Wildflowers of California, Nevada, and Arizona.* Albuquerque, NM: Jon Stewart Photography, 1998.

Tartan, M. *Tiny Explorers: Into the Wild: Outdoor Activities, Play Ideas and Fun.* London, UK: Miro Tartan, 2020.

Willis, K. J., and Katie Scott. *Botanicum.* Somerville, MA: Big Picture Press, 2017.

Zommer, Yuval. *The Big Book of Blooms.* New York, NY: Thames & Hudson, Inc., 2020.

For Mom and Dad, who helped me bloom. —L.K.

To Marc, Ian and Deirdre, for their support
and inspiration. —L.P.B.

Text © 2022 by Lisa Kerr
Illustrations © 2022 by Lisa Powell Braun

Edited by Michelle McCann

Library of Congress Cataloging-in-Publication Data

Names: Kerr, Lisa D., 1980- author. | Braun, Lisa Powell, illustrator.
Title: Wake, sleepy one : California poppies and the super bloom /
    written by Lisa Kerr ; illustrated by Lisa Powell Braun.
Description: Berkeley : West Margin Press, [2022] | Audience:
    Ages 4-8 | Audience: Grades K-1 | Summary: "A lyrical journey
    following the California poppy flower's life cycle from seed to
    super bloom, with sidebar information plus more details on the
    flowers at the back of the book"-- Provided by publisher.
Identifiers: LCCN 2021046242 (print) | LCCN 2021046243 (ebook) |
    ISBN 9781513128689 (hardback) | ISBN 9781513128696 (ebook)
Subjects: LCSH: California poppy--Juvenile literature.
Classification: LCC QK495.P22 K47 2022 (print) | LCC QK495.P22
    (ebook) | DDC 583/.35--dc23/eng/20211006
LC record available at https://lccn.loc.gov/2021046242
LC ebook record available at https://lccn.loc.gov/2021046243

Printed in the United States of America
26 25 24 23 2 3 4 5 6

Published by

WEST
MARGIN
PRESS

An imprint of Turner Publishing Company
WestMarginPress.com
TurnerBookstore.com

Proudly distributed by Ingram Publisher Services

WEST MARGIN PRESS
Publishing Director: Jennifer Newens
Marketing Manager: Alice Wertheimer
Project Specialist: Micaela Clark
Editor: Olivia Ngai
Design & Production: Rachel Lopez Metzger

Very special thanks to Jean Rhyne at
California State Parks for her time and
input on this book; Dr. Philip W. Rundel,
professor of Ecology and Evolutionary
Biology at UCLA, for his expert review;
and Ann-Marie Benz and Maya Argaman
with the California Native Plant Society
for their feedback on the book. This book
is stronger for your contributions.